Where's the Gift?

Using Feedback to Work Smarter, Learn Faster and Avoid Disaster

Nigel J.A. Bristow
Michael-John Bristow

Change a Little, Gain a Lot

Distributed by Targeted Learning
www.targetedlearning.com

Contact the Authors:
Nigel@targetedlearning.com
MJ@targetedlearning.com
For Volume Discounts: see pg. 76

ISBN# 978-0-9741409-3-3
Printed in the United States of America by
LCI Press, Orem, Utah
Cover Design—Bristow/Jones Marketing

To our colleagues, clients,
family and friends

"Love your enemies. They will tell you your faults."

—Benjamin Franklin

Table of Contents

Change a Little, Gain a Lot

Winston Churchill said, "Criticism may not be agreeable, but it is necessary. It fulfills the same function as pain in the human body. It calls attention to an unhealthy state of things." In short, we can't solve problems we don't see. Whether at home or in the workplace, that can lead to disaster.

A Personal Journey

No one is a stranger to the importance of feedback, myself included. This book was born twenty-five years ago, soon after I left South Africa to attend graduate school in the USA. I brought with me a strong competitive spirit and a determination to graduate in the top ten percent of my class. Consequently, I didn't hesitate to fully engage in class discussions and debates.

My favorite first-semester class focused on interpersonal skills. One afternoon, during a discussion on giving feedback, a fellow student turned to me and declared, in front of the entire class, "The problem with you is that you love the sound of your own voice."

Ouch! The fact that it was delivered for all to hear compounded my embarrassment. To be honest, I was tempted to punch him—but it was an interpersonal skills class, so I bit my tongue instead.

Although I consciously avoided appearing defensive, I mounted a valiant defense in my head. *He's wrong*, I remember telling myself. *He just wants to embarrass me in front of my peers.* I went home that night and told my wife about the incident. I expected understanding. I expected her to tell me he was wrong, that I was just doing my part in the course and that other students should step up if they didn't like it. I expected her to reinflate my ego.

I was mistaken.

When I told her what my classmate had said, her only comment was, "And that surprised you?"

Try as I might to dismiss what had happened, the sting of the original feedback, as well as my wife's comment, wouldn't let me forget. Eventually, I had to consider, *What if there are other classmates who see me the same way?*

Soon after, my anger cooled and I began to try a different approach in class discussions. I stopped being the first one to voice an opinion; I started listening more. Because of my competitive nature, I found it something of a challenge, but the results spurred me on. The quieter students began participating more in class and I discovered that they often made the most insightful comments. I'd like to think they were pleased with the change I had made. The truth is, I was the primary beneficiary; I learned more when I listened more. I changed a little and gained a lot.

The criticism I got twenty-five years ago helped me enormously. It taught me that leaders who listen more, talk less and let others voice their opinions before voicing their own get a lot more creativity, ownership and productivity from those around them. And because the criticism I received was delivered so poorly, it helped me understand that *all* feedback has the power to help us reach our goals – regardless of how it's delivered.

Feedback Defined

We define feedback as, "Information about your behavior or performance that can help you align your actions with your goals." Sometimes this information will sound like a reminder, a suggestion or helpful advice. At other times it may come across as criticism, a rebuke or even an insult. Regardless of its form, feedback can help you make better decisions about how to reach your goals.

Feedback and Your Own Learning Experience

Consider your own learning experiences. Can you think of a single skill you've mastered without feedback? No matter the skill, feedback played a role. That feedback may have come from another person, or even from the task itself; if you fell while learning to ride a bicycle, your feedback was a skinned knee. Whether learning to walk or talk or perform open-heart surgery, feedback is crucial to success.

We have all heard the phrase, "Practice makes perfect." Practice doesn't make perfect—it only makes permanent. We each have bad habits. How did they become permanent? Practice! To achieve mastery in anything, practice alone is insufficient. Only practice *plus* feedback make perfect.

Although experience has always been the best teacher, it instructs only those who take the time to extract its lessons. In the absence of feedback, the humility to hear it, the will to reflect on it, or the good sense to act on it, twenty years of experience are reduced to one year of experience repeated twenty times.

What the Research Says

Let's review a few research studies that confirm the strong link between feedback and success.

In his book <u>Talent is Overrated,</u> Geoff Colvin reports on dozens of studies that were designed to identify the path leading to world-class performance. The findings are conclusive: intensive practice along with constant feedback and adaptation—not innate talent or IQ—best explain exceptional performance.[1]

This is an empowering discovery. Becoming world class at something is not determined by an accident of birth, but is driven by individual choice that is informed by feedback. Your success is not determined by things over which you have little control, but is driven by abilities that are relatively easy to learn.

Seeking feedback also enhances how you are perceived by others. Ashford and Northcroft found that individuals who genuinely seek candid feedback are more highly valued by their managers than those who simply wait for feedback to come to them.[2]

Feedback is critical not just for personal success, but also for organization success. Research by Chris Voss of the London Business School demonstrates that customer satisfaction scores are highest for companies in which employees receive timely feedback directly from customers.[3] Information from daily, face-to-face customer feedback is more effective at improving customer satisfaction than information from annual customer service surveys. Timely feedback is the surest path to customer retention.

In his study of innovation, Gifford Pinchot found that successful innovators within large corporations are masters at seeking and using feedback. Before trying to secure formal sanction for their proposals, innovators informally solicit feedback from potential stakeholders and others. This allows them to identify and then plug holes in their new ideas—before trying to win broader support. By using feedback from potential critics to improve their ideas, the innovators transform potential naysayers into staunch supporters.[4]

Fearing criticism, some would-be innovators skip the above step. When they fail they blame it on "resistance to change"—when it was in reality their own "resistance to feedback" that derailed them. William Simms recognized the crippling power of fear: "Those who want to acquire fame and fortune must not show themselves afraid of criticism. The dread of criticism is the death of genius."

Even the most talented people need regular feedback to reach their potential. Kaplan and Kaiser studied people who had previously been identified as "high potentials." Some lived up to their promise. Others met with personal disaster such as being fired. Those who derailed were almost always tripped up by the same barrier: inadequate feedback.[5] In the absence of candid feedback—or because of their failure to hear it—these talented people continued to bank on their impressive strengths and largely ignore their blind spots. Over time, a valuable strength such as intelligence can devolve into a career derailer such as the inability to work well with others. As previously mentioned, people can't solve problems they don't see.

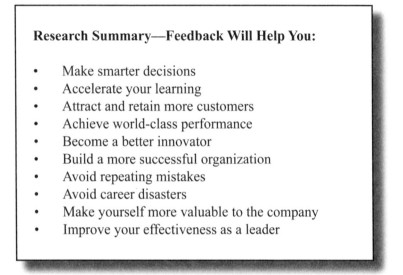

Research Summary—Feedback Will Help You:

- Make smarter decisions
- Accelerate your learning
- Attract and retain more customers
- Achieve world-class performance
- Become a better innovator
- Build a more successful organization
- Avoid repeating mistakes
- Avoid career disasters
- Make yourself more valuable to the company
- Improve your effectiveness as a leader

Your Path to World-Class Performance

Trying to achieve world-class performance without feedback is like playing golf in a dense fog; it's neither satisfying nor effective. Feedback lifts the fog and puts control back in your hands. Never fear feedback. Fear its absence.

With this in mind, let's turn to Matt, our fictional friend. In the following chapters we will follow Matt as he overcomes his fears and learns to find the gift in all feedback. At the end of each chapter, we have included a few case studies to illustrate the power of feedback and highlight some of the principles in Matt's story.

[1] Geoff Colvin, "*Talent Is Overrated: What Really Separates World-Class Performers from Everybody Else*," The Penguin Group, 2008.

[2] S.J. Ashford and G.B. Northcroft, "*Conveying More [or Less] Than We Realize: The Role of Impressions Management in Feedback Seeking*," Organizational Behavior and Human Decision Process, 1992, vol. 53.

[3] Chris Voss, London Business School, *The Economist*, April 24, 2004, p. 69.

[4] Gifford Pinchot III, "*Intrapreneuring: Why You Don't Have to Leave the Corporation to Become an Entrepreneur*," Harper and Row, 1985.

[5] R.E. Kaplan and R.B. Kaiser, "*Developing Versatile Leadership*," MIT Sloan Management Review, 44 (4), 2003.

How the Hippo Lost His Hair

"Those who venture to criticize us perform a remarkable act of friendship, for to undertake to wound or offend a man for his own good is to have a healthy regard for him."

—*Michel Eyquem de Montaigne*

Matt marched into Paula's office, visibly shaken. "I've been trying—I really have—but I'm not sure I can take this much longer," he said, waving a fistful of crumpled papers in the air. "Jalee is incredibly critical, but that's not the worst part. I could probably handle her constant badgering if she didn't keep swooping down on me like some corporate Genghis Khan." He slumped into an empty chair.

Paula, Matt's mentor at the company for the last six months, eased her glasses from her nose and eyed Matt with concern. She rose and closed the door, hushing the cacophony of noises from the corridor. Taking the seat next to Matt, she asked, "Okay, what happened?"

Matt took a breath and spilled the whole story. According to Jalee, his reports could have been sharper. His computer desktop was disorganized. He needed to walk faster to and from the restroom. Just last week she told him his socks didn't match.

Paula chuckled and Matt couldn't help but smile a little, too. He enjoyed talking through work problems with Paula. Four years his senior, she had a seasoned perspective but a fledgling's enthusiasm. She was an excellent listener, told great stories, and was often able to find the perfect quote to help him see his problems more clearly. By tapping into her experience and using her as a sounding board, Matt could usually arrive at a useful solution. This time was different. After ten minutes of explaining the situation to Paula, Matt still had no idea how to deal with his tactless manager. Recounting her constant nagging and apparent lack of interpersonal skills only made him angrier. When he finally finished, winded and flushed, Paula nodded. "Okay," she said.

"Okay?"

Paula stood and reached for a well-worn book on her shelf. "I've got a meeting, so we'll have to continue this later. In the meantime, there's an old African folktale at the beginning of this book that you might find useful. It's short, so give it a read today and we can talk again soon."

"When?" Matt looked worried, his eyebrows crumpled like the forgotten papers clutched in his hand.

"Tomorrow," she said. "Breakfast. Seven-thirty in the cafeteria. We'll figure this out."

Matt nodded and took the book. He studied the cracked leather cover. The title was faded and barely legible. "Ancient African Folktales for the Modern Business World." He thanked Paula. She waved it away with a smile and they parted company. As soon as he got to his office, Matt began reading.

How the Hippo Lost His Hair

The first hippopotamus to walk the earth was not hairless like the hippos of today. He had a beautiful fur coat and a mane so thick it was rivaled only by that of the lion. Although his coat had been inherited from his ancestors, Hippo took full credit for its beauty and luster and showed it off whenever he could. In fact, Hippo would grow quite ill-tempered at night because the darkness hid his coat from the envious glances of the other animals.

Thanks to his elegant fur, Hippo didn't need to sleep near the fire like the others—his coat kept him warm. Even so, each night Hippo would lie just a little closer to the flames. He wanted the light from the fire to shine on his fur so everyone could admire it twenty-four hours a day.

One evening Lion gave Hippo a gentle warning, suggesting softly that it might not be safe to sleep so close to the fire. Hippo ignored him. "Lion is just jealous," he thought. "Jealous because all the animals can see both day and night that my coat is better than his."

Jackal was also worried about Hippo's coat catching fire. Jackal, however, despite her great intellect, did not have great tact. "You big hairy oaf," grated Jackal. "Your inflated pride is matched only by your girth, and it's going to get you into trouble one of these days."

Hippo was indignant. "I didn't ask for her opinion! How dare she speak to me like that. When she learns how to treat me with respect, I will listen."

One night disaster struck. Hippo slept just a little too close to the fire. A stray spark flew into his fur and his exquisite coat burst into flames. Hippo made a desperate dash for the river, but by the

*time he got there it was too late. Although he
couldn't see it in the darkness, his fur was gone.
He spent the rest of the night in the cool waters
of the river.*

*When the sun rose the next morning, Hippo
climbed onto the riverbank and shook himself off.
He turned to admire his reflection in the water.
Instead of a thick glossy coat, Hippo saw only
charred flesh.*

*"If only I had listened to Lion, or even Jackal!"
he wailed, then immediately plunged back into the
water. To this day, to hide his embarrassment,
Hippo spends the sunlit hours buried in the waters
of the river. Only at night does he venture out,
when he can eat without worrying who might
catch a glimpse of his hideous hairless hide.*

Matt and Paula met the next morning in the cafeteria as planned.
Paula jumped right in. "What do you think of the story?"

Matt had the book in his hands. He wagged it at Paula, feigning
disapproval. "I think this folktale is your crafty way of giving me
feedback. Honestly, it stung a bit. Yesterday my complaints about
Jalee's lack of tact seemed perfectly reasonable. Yet when Hippo
in the story said virtually the same thing about Jackal, it sounded
pretty lame."

"How so?"

"If Hippo hadn't dismissed Jackal's blunt advice, he could have
kept his coat. Maybe I'm a bit like the hippo. If the feedback
isn't what I consider 'constructive', I'm inclined to get defensive

and dismiss it." Matt leaned forward. "That said, Jalee's my supervisor. The company executives always say that employees are our most important asset; 'respect the individual' is in our values statement. As someone in a position of authority, Jalee should know how to give feedback in a more constructive way."

Paula nodded. "Maybe, but clearly she doesn't. In reality, you have virtually no direct control over how Jalee gives you feedback. What you *do* control is how you receive it—and using that control wisely makes all the difference.

"When I first started working here, my supervisor taught me to think of feedback as a gift. When I complained about some tactless customer or team member, he'd tell me not to throw away the gift just because I didn't like the wrapping. I try to remind myself that there's always a gift hidden in the feedback. It may take some digging, but it's in there.

"Let me give you a real-life example of someone who excelled at this. Abraham Lincoln was the opposite of Hippo. When Lincoln was running for President, one of his greatest detractors was Edwin Stanton, a rather arrogant and tactless man—very similar to the jackal in the story. Stanton did not like Lincoln at all, and the relationship became only more strained after Lincoln won the presidency. Despite Stanton's shortcomings, he was both smart and candid, so Lincoln appointed him Secretary of War.

"One day a congressman asked Lincoln to sign a certain proposal. Lincoln read the proposal, liked it and signed it. He told the congressman to take it to Stanton and get his signature as well. The congressman visited Stanton and gave him the proposal. Stanton read it and expressed in no uncertain terms that he thought the proposal was stupid. The congressman explained that the President himself had approved it. Stanton said, 'Lincoln approved this? Then he's a damned fool.'

"You can imagine the congressman went back to Lincoln in a real hurry, explaining that Stanton wouldn't sign the proposal. Lincoln asked if Stanton knew that he, the president, had approved it. The congressman affirmed and Lincoln asked, 'What did he say?'

"A little uncomfortably, the congressman answered, 'Well, sir, he called you a damned fool.'

"Lincoln sat in silence for a moment. Then he stood and said, 'If Stanton said I was a damned fool, then I must be one, for he is nearly always right and generally says what he means. I will step over and see him.'

"When Lincoln took office, he brought with him less experience than almost any other president—before or since—yet historians consider him one of the greatest presidents in U.S. history. What made him great was his ability to put his ego aside and learn from others. Stanton was smart; Lincoln was smarter. Lincoln knew he could learn a lot more from candid people than he could from those who always tried to protect his feelings, or who were afraid to speak frankly because he was in a position of power. After talking with Stanton, Lincoln withdrew his support for the proposal.

"When I was asked to be a mentor here, I was told my role wasn't to put into the mentee what nature left out, but to build on what nature had already put in. Let's talk about your situation. What did nature leave out of Jalee? What are her weaknesses?"

"I'd say interpersonal skills."

"Okay. What are her strengths?"

Matt thought for a moment and then admitted, a bit grudgingly, "I suppose she has pretty good analytical skills…and a keen eye for spotting issues that might become problems down the road."

"Great. Think of Jalee as your second pair of eyes. She sometimes sees problems you don't. And you can't solve problems you don't see. Also, like Stanton, she's a straight talker. Make her strengths your new focus. Just as Lincoln saw past Stanton's lack of humility and tact, try looking beyond Jalee's shortcomings. Center instead on how her talents can help you master your job more quickly. I know that's easier said than done, but it's worth the effort."

"So rather than wishing she were more diplomatic, I should take advantage of her candor? I still wish she could be nicer about it." Matt silently wondered if this was going to be worth the effort but agreed to give it a try.

"One more thing," Paula said. "What about the lion in the story? Hippo also rejected Lion's warnings, even though Lion was very diplomatic."

"I didn't pay much attention to Lion," Matt said. He opened the book and skimmed the story again. "You're right. It says the lion warned the hippo 'gently' and 'softly'—perfectly constructive. It seems Hippo didn't have a problem with the wrapping but with the messenger. He saw Lion as a competitor, and an inferior one at that, so he was suspicious of Lion's motives and ignored the warning." Matt paused. "I don't think that's my problem with Jalee. With her it's the wrapping."

"I agree. It doesn't specifically relate to your challenge with Jalee, but it's something to keep in mind in case you get feedback from someone you're not sure you can trust, or from people who aren't as capable as you. They still have a valuable perspective and there's a gift to find in that."

"So the two things I get from the story are: don't throw the gift away just because you don't like the wrapping, and don't throw it away because you don't like—or respect—the person giving it."

"I'd say that sums it up."

On their way out of the cafeteria Paula said, "Good luck. Let me know how it goes with Jalee, or with anyone else, for that matter."

Matt returned to his office and decided to record his thoughts. From the top drawer of his desk he grabbed the worn spiral notebook he used as a journal and wrote:

Feedback is a gift.

You can't solve problems you don't see. Feedback gives you additional pairs of eyes.

Don't discard the gift because you don't like the wrapping.

Don't reject the gift because you don't like or respect the giver—or because you suspect their motives.

It may be more comfortable working with diplomats, but you learn a lot more from straight talkers.

The Truth Shall Set You Free

Andreas Treichl is the head of Erste Bank, the second largest bank in Austria. One measure of his success is the fact that Erste Bank escaped the worst of the 2008/2009 global financial crisis by keeping "their strategies simple and their ambitions relatively modest."[1]

Earlier in life, Andreas Treichl had ambitions to become an orchestra conductor—a path which changed course after Leonard Bernstein watched him perform. The famous conductor, reports Mr. Treichl, recommended that he "go into banking because one would do better as a mediocre banker than one would as a mediocre conductor."

Since Mr. Treichl obviously has the talents to do significantly better than "mediocre" as a banker, both fields—conducting and banking—benefited from Mr. Bernstein's timely and candid feedback. We are also confident that Mr. Treichl is more fulfilled as a first-rate banker than he would have been as a second-rate conductor.

Although Andreas Treichl gives Leonard Bernstein credit for helping him avoid a potential career disaster, he can take some credit for himself; he was smart enough to listen to feedback that must have been very painful at the time.

Over the past decade our company, Targeted Learning, has asked thousands of people to describe the most helpful criticism they've ever received. Of those, over 75% responded that their immediate reaction to that feedback was negative. They reported a range of painful feelings, including disappointment, annoyance, sadness, shock, anger and even betrayal. As Thomas Fuller observed, "The sting of criticism is the truth of it." It is not always easy to see ourselves as others see us.

Because most people in our study reported a negative initial reaction to being given candid feedback, it's easy to wonder how so many of them came to see it as the most helpful feedback of their entire lives. Apparently, the gift in the feedback was found not in spite of the pain, but precisely because of it. Paradoxically, it is often the pain in criticism that causes us to reflect on the message long enough to discover the gift in it. The people who should be concerned are not those who feel pain when criticized; rather, it is those who don't feel much at all.

At one of our mentoring workshops, an oil rig supervisor reminded us, "The truth will set you free. But first it's going to hurt like hell."[2]

[1] *The Economist*, September 5, 2009, p. 74.
[2] Paul Nash, Oil Rig Supervisor, 2009.

Improving Health and Safety at Work

"I'm a medical doctor in a health clinic. We set a goal to dramatically decrease the rate at which our staff contracted illnesses from patients. Using gloves and washing and sanitizing hands more frequently helped, but it didn't give us the dramatic improvements we wanted.

"Bacteria and viruses can only make one sick by entering the body, which cannot happen through unbroken skin. The primary entry points for germs are the eyes, nose and mouth. We were finally successful when, in addition to the standard procedures for keeping hands clean, we got people to stop touching their faces. Getting people to wash their hands and wear gloves is comparatively easy to do. The problem with touching our faces is that we all do it dozens of times a day, and ninety percent of the time we are not even aware we are doing it.

"To change people's ingrained habits we made giving feedback an expectation of every staff member. If you saw someone rubbing their chin, scratching their nose, or touching any other part of their face, you had to immediately bring it to their attention. No exceptions. That meant nurses and receptionists were required to give feedback not only to their peers, but to the doctors as well. This was difficult because most of the staff were uncomfortable giving feedback to doctors, and doctors were not traditionally open to criticism from non-doctors. It took some time, but we persisted. Eventually we changed the culture and infections dropped dramatically."

— General Practitioner, Intermountain Instacare

When it comes to changing ingrained habits, immediate feedback is the key. If staff members had received monthly reports telling them how many times they had touched their faces in the previous 30 days, little would have changed. What made this effort successful was that people were given feedback right at the moment when their hands were in contact with their faces. In time, people became more self-aware of their habit and could catch themselves in the act. Soon people started catching themselves before the act, and only then could new habits displace the old.

The moral of the story: If you want to break a bad habit, your shortest and surest path to success is to license others to give you feedback at the moment they see you succumbing to your habit. And if you want to entrench a new value in the culture of your company, you need to license individuals at every level to give feedback to people at any level, whenever they see behavior that contradicts that value.

The health clinic described in this case created what we call a "Feedback Culture." A feedback culture is one where people feel safe giving candid feedback, because those who receive it have the skills and responsibility to receive it as a gift. Any company that is serious about safety, or any other value for that matter, needs a feedback culture to secure that value.

Gift Wrapped

"If in the last few years you haven't discarded a major opinion or acquired a new one, check your pulse. You may be dead."

—*Gelett Burgess*

A few days later, Paula stopped by Matt's office. "Hey, if you've got a minute, I have a gift in my office that I'd like to give you," she said.

"Ah. A *gift*." Matt nodded knowingly.

Paula grinned and shook her head. "No, not feedback. The old-fashioned kind. You responded so well to the hippo story that I thought you might appreciate it. Walk with me to my office."

Matt fell into step. "I have a question," he said. "What if the person giving you feedback is basing it on incorrect information? It seems like it would be dangerous to act on every bit of feedback you receive."

"It could be very dangerous. You should seldom, if ever, take feedback purely at face value. Sometimes feedback will be inaccurate, either because the person giving it is out of touch with the situation or they don't have certain crucial information. That doesn't mean the feedback can't be of value.

"Let me share a personal example. A few years ago, a colleague from another group approached me and accused me of failing to meet my commitments. That wasn't true; I had met every commitment he referred to and I could prove it. But I still learned something from the feedback."

"To ignore it?"

Paula smiled. "If only it were that easy. The gift actually came from trying to figure out how this guy reached his incorrect conclusion. I knew I was meeting my commitments, but I realized I had failed to keep him informed. So I started working harder at keeping him and others in the loop about my work. It made a huge difference. Now I actually consider his feedback some of the most helpful I've ever received, even though it was based on faulty information—quite the paradox. I found out that you can learn as much, if not more, from others' inaccurate perceptions as you can from their accurate ones.

"People say that what you don't know can't hurt you, but that's a dangerous assumption. If you're diligent, smart and honest, your career is more likely to be derailed by inaccurate perceptions than by accurate ones. And if you don't know what those *inaccurate* perceptions are, you're powerless to change them."

They reached Paula's office. She motioned Matt to go in first and pointed towards a box on her desk. It was a large box, about two feet tall, dented, torn in several places, and covered in dark smudges. Matt, looking puzzled, picked it up and saw his name scribbled carelessly over the top. "I have no idea what's in here, but thank you."

Paula just smiled.

"Can I open it now?" he asked. She nodded.

The box was filled with shredded newspaper. Matt pulled some out, examined it, then returned it to the box. He repeated this several times before realizing he was just recycling through the garbage at the top of the box. After pulling out the paper and setting it in a pile on the desk, he found a shoebox.

Matt's expectant smile disappeared when he opened it and realized that it too was filled with shredded newspaper. He shrugged and resumed the search. By now Paula's desk was buried in paper. Finally Matt found it: a small, intricately carved wooden hippo.

He picked up the carving. "This is great! I'll keep it on my desk to remind me of Hippo's fate. Thank you."

"You're welcome. You probably noticed there was a metaphor within this metaphor."

"Yep. The wrapping was pretty scrappy even though there really was a gift inside, just like feedback that might be helpful even if the delivery is terrible."

"True. To find the value in all feedback you have to first overlook the disagreeable packaging it often comes in. Was there anything else you had to overlook?"

"Yes, all that shredded paper. While I was going through it I kept wondering, 'Where's the gift?' I probably asked it a dozen times before I actually found the hippo. That's the kind of question I should ask myself the next time Jalee gives me poorly-wrapped feedback."

"What does the shredded paper—the garbage—represent in a feedback discussion?"

"It could be outdated or questionable information that isn't very useful. The key is to examine it and figure out where it came from, like you did when that guy said you weren't meeting your commitments. You set the questionable scraps aside and kept digging. And in my case, until I took the shredded newspaper out of the box and set it aside, I wasn't going to find the gift."

"Good connection," said Paula. "When we get feedback that appears harsh, or is based on inaccurate perceptions, and we fight it by saying, 'That's not right,' or, 'That's not fair,' or, 'She's doing this to hurt me,' we're just recycling the garbage in our heads, along with our own prejudices. As long as we continue to do that, finding the gift is impossible. So what gets in the way of *you* finding the gifts from Jalee?"

Matt thought for a while. Eventually he said, "One piece of garbage that I probably recycle when Jalee criticizes me is that she doesn't like me. I can see how that makes it difficult for me to find any gifts in her feedback."

"In the future, give her the benefit of the doubt. Candid feedback is rarely reliable evidence that someone doesn't like you. In fact, people who don't care about you are just as likely to treat you with indifference or silence—they don't take the time to give you feedback at all. It's like Socrates once said: 'Think not those faithful who praise all thy words and actions, but those who kindly reprove thy faults.' "

"When the 'kindly' part is missing, it's hard for me to feel the caring," said Matt, smiling.

"I know what you mean. It won't be easy, but really push yourself to view Jalee's honesty as potential evidence of caring. I guarantee it'll make a big difference."

"So what you're telling me is to get over it. Jalee can be a source of real help whether she likes me or not."

Paula smiled, "That's it exactly."

Matt returned to his office, wooden hippo in hand. That afternoon, a friend noticed it sitting on his desk and Matt told the story about opening the gift. That got Matt thinking. After his friend left, Matt compared finding the hippo to the times he had found value in criticism. He identified the similarities and created his own process for receiving feedback:

Four Steps to Receiving the Gift of Feedback

1. **Acknowledge the Gift.**

   Say thank you; give the giver the benefit of the doubt.

   Assume there is something of value.

2. **Open the Gift.**

   Sometimes the gift is hard to find; it takes digging.

   To find it, ask lots of questions and listen with an open mind.

3. **Confirm the Nature and Value of the Gift.**

   Put into words what you understand the gift to be.

   If you can, mention how you plan to use it.

4. **Use the Gift.**

   After using it—and experiencing its benefits—let the giver know how it helped you.

Matt studied his list, then returned to the principles he had written a few days earlier. Matt found the one that stated, "Feedback is a gift" and added to it. He then inserted a few additional principles:

Feedback is a gift—even when it's inaccurate.

To find the gift, ask yourself questions such as:

> **Where's the gift?**
>
> **What can I learn from this?**
>
> **What did I do or say that may have created this misperception?**
>
> **What can I do to ensure this doesn't happen again?**

Continue asking these questions until you find the gift.

When you encounter inaccurate information, unfair conclusions, etc., examine it carefully, set it aside—along with your own prejudices—and keep digging.

Feedback and Airline Disasters

On January 13, 1982, Air Florida Flight 90 lost altitude almost immediately after taking off from Washington National Airport and crashed into the frozen Potomac River. The National Transportation Safety Board concluded that the tragedy was caused by two factors: ice-covered wings and insufficient power to the engines. The NTSB final report stated that Flight 90 could have taken off safely if only one of those factors was present, but the combined effect was devastating.

During takeoff the cockpit instruments indicated that the engines were producing the required amount of power, but ice on the probe that measured engine power caused a false reading. The engines were in reality only producing 70 percent of the necessary power.

As the plane accelerated down the runway, the first officer realized something was wrong. The plane wasn't accelerating as fast as it should have been. The first officer recognized the discrepancy between the two sources of feedback (the rate of acceleration and the instrument reading) and expressed his concern to the captain.

In the space of only 21 seconds, the first officer questioned the instrument reading an alarming four times. The captain, relying only on the instruments, disregarded the feedback from his first officer and chose not to abort the takeoff. As a result, seventy-eight people lost their lives.

What is particularly instructive in this case was that the so-called "objective readings" from the instruments were wrong, while the so-called "subjective perceptions" of the first officer were right.

In his book "Outliers," Malcolm Gladwell[1] notes an anomaly in commercial plane disasters. Although captains and first officers split flying duties equally, a higher percentage of crashes have historically occurred when the captain (i.e., the more experienced pilot) was at the controls. The research of Fischer and Orasanu[2] explains this anomaly. They studied communication patterns in the cockpit and found that when the captain was at the controls, the less experienced first officer was reluctant to speak frankly. But when the first officer was at the controls, the captain felt no such constraint.

The NTSB report on the crash of Air Florida Flight 90 encouraged airlines to focus on improving communication and openness within the cockpit. The airlines have worked hard to create a culture where crew members feel comfortable giving timely and clear feedback to each other, especially to the captain. For example, to reduce the barrier of rank, some airlines now insist that the flight crew address the captain by his or her first name rather than the title of "captain." These and many other efforts have resulted in a significant improvement in airline safety.

[1] Malcolm Gladwell, *"Outliers: The Story of Success,"* Little, Brown and Company, 2008.

[2] U. Fischer and J. Orasanu, *"Cultural Diversity and Crew Communication,"* presented at the 50th Astronautical Congress, Amsterdam, October 1999.

You're Not at University Anymore

"The most valuable criticism I ever received was right at the beginning of my career. I had written my first technical report and was fully expecting accolades from my manager. After reviewing the report, my manager called me into her office and told me, 'You're not at university anymore,' then promptly threw my report in the trash.

"I was shocked; she certainly got my attention. Figuring out where I'd gone wrong became my top priority, so I immediately asked her a lot of questions. What I learned was that the approach to report writing that had earned me A's at university totally missed the mark in the corporate world. I learned that managers used technical reports to make business decisions, not to assess the intellectual horsepower of subordinates. They didn't want a detached academic analysis of the situation. They wanted me to have a point of view and to make specific and well-reasoned recommendations. That feedback, as tactless as it was, taught me more about what I needed to do to get ahead in my career than an entire year in graduate school."

—A Fidelity Investments manager participating in
Targeted Learning's "Mentoring Skills" Workshop

Although we do not condone throwing people's reports into the trash, this case does reinforce something we've noted about many of the most effective mentors we've met: they have high standards and are not shy about telling you when you fall short of their expectations. As in this case, they might not always be as tactful or as clear as you would like—in fact, "curmudgeon" is a much better description of some of these mentors than "diplomat"—but you always know when there is a problem that needs attention and closer investigation.

When given harsh or unkind feedback, most people take offense. Smart people take notes. The individual in this case understood the key to differentiating oneself: what you learn in the classroom is available to everyone, so it's what you learn outside the classroom that really sets you apart.

Back on the Farm

*"Criticism is something we can avoid easily by
saying nothing, doing nothing, and being nothing."*

—*Aristotle*

Matt visited Paula in her office a few days later. "Thanks again
for the wooden hippo," he said. "It's a constant reminder to me
to treat all feedback as a gift."

"Glad to hear it. So what have you done?"

"I looked at the steps I followed when I received your gift and
I also considered other times I've learned from criticism. From
that I created my own process for receiving feedback and I've
started using it with Jalee."

"Even better!"

Matt continued, "Since changing my approach, I'm amazed how
much more I've been able to learn from her. Whenever she gives
me feedback with her trademark bluntness, I try to think of it as a
game—I win whenever I find the gift in her message. So far, I'm
five for five."

"That's great. Now what's this miraculous process?"

Matt handed her a typed copy of the four steps. "I start simply
with, 'Thanks for bringing this to my attention.' Then I tell Jalee
something like, 'I'd really like to understand this.' I follow with
some questions and really focus on listening to her response. I
find it easier to listen openly if I keep asking myself things like,

'Where's the gift? What can I learn from this? What did I do that might have created this perception?' When I think I've found the gift, I summarize it for Jalee and ask if I missed anything. It's worked like a charm so far."

"How has it affected your overall relationship with Jalee?"

"I've already noticed the quality of her feedback improving. Now that she knows I take it seriously, she seems to be giving it with more clarity and less, well, intensity than she did before."

"That sounds like real progress." Paula held up Matt's typed list. "Just give me a moment to read through your model."

Matt watched her read and thought she looked pretty pleased. He was right. "Matt, this model of yours is excellent," Paula said. "There are two pieces here that I've never really considered before: the part in Step 3, about mentioning how you plan to use the feedback; then, in Step 4, telling the person how it has helped you. These will definitely help keep the door open for more feedback in the future."

"Glad you like it. I confess that when I started working on the list, I didn't really think it would yield much. But by the time I was finished I was feeling pretty good about it. Speaking of feedback, any thoughts on how I could improve it?"

Paula looked through the list again. "Nothing big. I might add a point at the end of Step 2 about not explaining yourself. The moment you start explaining, you stop learning. Even the most legitimate explanation will sound like an excuse. It only makes you sound defensive."

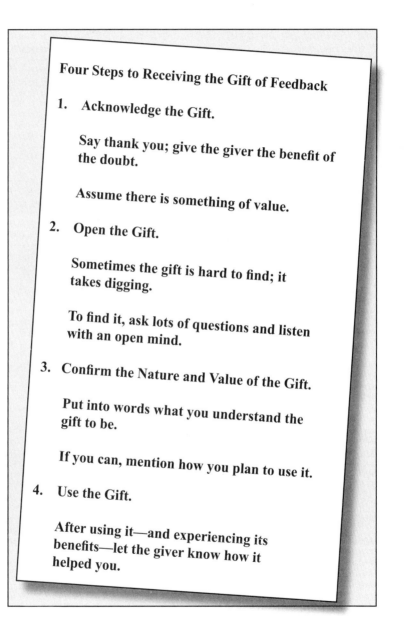

Four Steps to Receiving the Gift of Feedback

1. Acknowledge the Gift.

   Say thank you; give the giver the benefit of the doubt.

   Assume there is something of value.

2. Open the Gift.

   Sometimes the gift is hard to find; it takes digging.

   To find it, ask lots of questions and listen with an open mind.

3. Confirm the Nature and Value of the Gift.

   Put into words what you understand the gift to be.

   If you can, mention how you plan to use it.

4. Use the Gift.

   After using it—and experiencing its benefits—let the giver know how it helped you.

"That makes sense. Thanks. There's something else I'm struggling with. I like the idea of feedback as a gift, so I've been asking people other than Jalee for feedback. But all I usually get is, 'You're doing fine. Just keep it up,' or something equally vague. What do I do when people are reluctant to give me specific feedback?"

"Why do you think they might be reluctant?"

"I guess most folks are afraid of conflict, so they avoid saying anything that might sound critical—which, by the way, is the polar opposite of Jalee. I used to think her blunt feedback was unhelpful. I'm beginning to think that the most unhelpful feedback is no feedback at all."

"I agree. It can be frustrating when you make a mistake and someone gets on your case, but there's one thing that's even worse: when you make a mistake and no one says anything at all. It means they've given up on you completely; they don't think you're capable of anything better."

"That's a scary thought," Matt said.

"I think that's why Samuel Johnson claimed that he 'would rather be attacked than unnoticed.' Now, back to your concern about people being afraid to offer honest feedback. If that's the case, what can you do to make it safe for them to give it?"

"Somehow, I have to convince them that I really do want their feedback. I can tell them that I see its value and I won't be offended. Other than that, I'm not quite sure what I can do."

"It is important to communicate your openness and willing-ness to hear feedback," said Paula, "and it will work for a lot of people, but some may need a little more prodding.

"Here's a principle I learned from my grandfather. When I was growing up we often visited his farm in the summer. There was no running water in the house. All he had was an old manual pump in the backyard. One day, he asked me to go pump him a bowl of water. I went to the back and pumped as hard as I could but got nothing. I told my grandpa what happened and he laughed. He said the pump was like everything else in life—you have to put something in to get something out.

"He walked me back outside, picked up a bucket of water next to the house and poured some into the pump. I tried it again, and this time water came gushing out. He called it 'priming the pump.'

"I've found that sometimes if you want honest feedback, you have to prime the pump first with a little self-critique. Let's say you want to improve your facilitation skills and need some feedback. How would you prime the pump?"

"I could say, 'I need to improve my facilitation skills for our team meetings. What thoughts do you have on how I can be a better facilitator?' Is that what you mean by priming the pump?"

"You're 80 percent of the way there. People are more likely to see your sincerity if your self-critique is more specific."

"So something like, 'I'm working on improving my facilitation skills. One thing I've noticed is that I'm not very good at getting people involved. I think if I asked more questions, and gave people more time to respond, I would do a lot better. What else do you think I could do to get people involved?' Is that specific enough?"

Paula nodded. "That was perfect. I've noticed that when people come to me with some vague request for feedback like, 'How am I doing?' it sounds more like a request for validation. Lots of people ask for feedback, but more often than not, what they really want is a pat on the back. When you prime the pump, you let the other person know that you genuinely want to improve and you're not just looking for a warm fuzzy."

"But isn't there a danger in priming the pump? It seems like you would only get feedback on something you've already identified as an issue. Maybe the most important problem is something you're not even aware of."

"Excellent point. After I prime the pump, I like to make sure that I end the conversation by saying something like, 'Thank you so much. This has been very helpful. Do you have any other suggestions for me?'"

That sounded good to Matt, but he stopped her when she rose. "One more question. What if I get feedback I fundamentally disagree with? For example, what if someone tells me I should use more statistics in my presentations, and I genuinely believe I should use less?"

"Are you asking what you should do before or after you've asked your questions and summarized what they've said?"

"After."

She shrugged. "What do you think?"

"Honestly…I think I would have to set it aside," said Matt.

Paula nodded. "If you've made a genuine effort to understand the feedback, setting it aside may be the best thing to do. Remember, feedback is information that you use to help you reach your goals. If you think someone's suggestions will take you in the wrong direction, then you need to weigh the evidence and go with your best judgment. That said, you don't have enough evidence to judge wisely until you get input from a third—or even a fourth—party."

"You mean I should validate it with someone else?"

Paula hesitated. "Well, yes and no. Yes, you should get a second opinion from someone who is an accomplished presenter and will level with you. At the same time, how you frame your request will make a world of difference. For example, you could say, 'You won't believe it. Jack just told me that I should use more statistics in my presentation. What do you think?' But then all you're likely to get is validation of your own biases.

"On the other hand, you could say, 'This morning someone mentioned that I need to use more statistics in my presentation. The quality of my presentations is important to me. What are your thoughts on what I could do to make my presentations more powerful?'

"If they don't mention statistics, or—without any prompts from you—say that they disagree with the other person's suggestion, then you may choose to set the original advice aside. But if they suggest more statistics, then you need to explore how they think statistics could be used more effectively.

"My grandfather had a favorite quote that applies to this. It comes from Sholem Aleichem, a famous Yiddish author and playwright from the nineteenth century: 'If someone tells you you have ears like a donkey, pay no attention. But if two people tell you, buy yourself a saddle.'"

Matt laughed, "I think I would've liked your grandfather."

"You would have. I have another Lincoln story that I think will help answer your question."

"At the beginning of the Civil War the South consistently out-maneuvered the North. The Confederacy had some very talented generals and the Union just couldn't compete, until a man by the name of Ulysses S. Grant came on the scene. Grant was bold and a good tactician, and was soon appointed General-in-Chief of the Union forces. In short order, he turned the tide of the war.

"There was just one small problem. Grant enjoyed his whiskey a little too much. Lincoln caught a lot of flak for appointing Grant. 'How could you have this drunkard leading our forces?' people asked. Lincoln took that feedback and decided to examine it further; he sent a few agents from the war department on an undercover mission. They spent about three weeks in Grant's camp before reporting back to Lincoln. Upon their return they told Lincoln that Grant did indeed drink rather liberally, but he was still the best general they had ever seen.

"Based on that report, Lincoln kept Grant as General-in-Chief, although he continued to receive criticism regarding the hard-drinking general. Eventually Lincoln responded by telling the critics that if they could tell him the brand of Grant's favorite whiskey, Lincoln would give it to all his generals."

Matt chuckled before turning thoughtful. "So Lincoln set the feedback aside, but only after giving it due diligence."

"Yes. And even then, the feedback should still be considered a gift. In the end, Lincoln set the feedback aside, but he still identified a potential problem. He needed to continue to monitor the situation in case it changed for the worse."

"But what if you do your due diligence and still can't see any value in the feedback—now or in the future—do you tell them?"

"What do you do when you get a present from a friend that you can't use? Would you tell them, 'Thanks, but I don't need it'?"

"Never," replied Matt.

"Exactly; they'd be understandably hurt. When I get a less-than-useful gift, I take that gift and thank my friend for their thoughtfulness. I know the intent was to give me something of value so I should be genuinely thankful. Then I put the gift on the shelf, knowing that maybe I'll find a use for it down the road. Sometimes I use it later; sometimes I don't. But I never do anything to suggest I don't appreciate the gesture."

"So you're saying you've never regifted anything?" Matt teased.

"I'm going to plead the fifth on that," laughed Paula. "Let me clarify something I just said. There are exceptions to just putting someone's feedback on the shelf and leaving it at that. Sometimes feedback from a customer or supervisor is given in a way that implies an expectation that you'll take specific action. If you have done your due diligence, and still believe you cannot—or should not—comply with their request, you need to get back to them."

"How do you do that without coming across as defensive or dismissive?"

"That is a challenge. Start by summarizing what you learned from the feedback, and ask them if you accurately understood their concerns. When they confirm that you have, tell them why you take their feedback seriously. Then outline the process you followed to investigate their request or concern, and tell them what you learned. Close by summarizing your options, the pros and cons of each as you see them, and explain your decision in terms of how it best supports everyone's goals—theirs, the company's, and your own."

Later that day Matt added the following to his journal:

> **It's a really bad sign if you make a mistake and no
> one criticizes you. The most unhelpful feedback is no
> feedback at all.**
>
> **When asking for feedback, be specific about what you
> want and why you want it.**
>
> **Be ready to prime the pump with a specific self-
> critique.**
>
> **You don't have to agree with feedback to
> benefit from it. You only have to understand it.**
>
> **You can set feedback aside, but only after giving it
> due diligence.**
>
> **If feedback comes with the expectation that you will
> take action, you do have the right to set it aside, but
> you still need to let the person know your decision—
> and how you arrived at it.**

Then Matt added to his four-step model:

Four Steps to Receiving the Gift of Feedback

1. Acknowledge the Gift

2. Open the Gift

    Do NOT explain yourself.

3. Confirm the Nature and Value of the Gift

    Thank the person again and ask, "Is there anything else I could do to be more effective in the future?"

4. Use the Gift

    If you can't use the gift right now, say "thank you" and set it aside; you might find a use for it later.

    Before setting feedback aside, check in with someone you trust who will be honest with you.

When Bad Advice Can Be a Gift

"The most helpful criticism I ever received was while working at a local bank. I was eager to demonstrate my initiative, only to be reprimanded by my boss. He said, 'Look kid, if you hope to continue working at this bank, leave your initiative at home.'

"That criticism was immensely disappointing, but it prompted me to ask myself, 'Do I really want to work for a company that doesn't value initiative?' The answer was obvious, which led to the best career decision of my life. I quit as soon as I could find an employer who valued initiative.

"At the time I thought my boss was a jerk. I have since come to appreciate him for telling me an important truth about the culture of the company. Only in hindsight do I appreciate the favor he did for me."

—A ConocoPhillips manager participating in Targeted Learning's "Seven Conversations for Exceptional Leaders" Workshop

Shakespeare said, "Take each man's censure but reserve thy judgment." In other words, welcome criticism from anyone who cares to offer it, but don't jump to any premature conclusions. Sometimes the criticism may be valid. Sometimes not. You need to take some time to reflect on the criticism, and then decide for yourself what to do with it. In this particular case, the gift in the criticism did not come from what it said about the recipient. The gift was in the insight it gave the recipient into his boss' and the organization's values.

The Power of Identifying the Gift

Michael McCullough at the University of Miami conducted a study where 300 participants were asked to recall an insult or offense that had been eating away at them.[1] One third of these participants were asked to describe the event and how it had hurt them. Another third were asked to describe the event and something they gained or learned from it. The rest were asked to describe their plans for the next day. The follow-up assessment found that those who identified the gift in the event felt significantly more forgiving towards those who had offended them. They were less inclined than the other groups to seek revenge or to avoid those who had hurt them. This research confirms our own findings: Looking for the gift in feedback not only helps us learn more from our experiences; it also helps us build healthier relationships.

[1] M.E. McCullough, L.M. Root and A.D. Cohen, *"Writing About the Benefits of an Interpersonal Transgression Facilitates Forgiveness,"* Journal of Consulting and Clinical Psychology, *74, 887-897, 2006*

My Worst Manager Was Also the Nicest

"In my first job after graduation I worked for a wonderfully nice manager. He was one of the most positive people I've ever met. He would often compliment me on my work and offer words of encouragement. On a few occasions he called me into his office to ask how things were going. He would then praise me lavishly for something I'd done, followed by a suggestion that I try doing something differently. He always ended the conversation on a positive note by telling me how impressed he was with my progress. Given all the praise I was getting, my confidence and self-esteem were higher than they'd ever been—until the day he called me into his office and fired me for being unresponsive to his counseling. It's ironic. The manager who did me the greatest disservice was also the 'nicest' manager I've ever had."

—A former colleague of the authors

This person might have fared better had she been aware of this observation by Wilfred A. Peterson: "Critics wake us up. Kindness often covers up the truth and allows us to sleep on in our ignorance."

Although the manager in this case study did this individual an enormous disservice by failing to give her feedback in clear and unambiguous terms, she was partly responsible for her own demise—by not being savvy enough to realize that a manager's "suggestion" is almost always more than a suggestion. The question to ask oneself is: why do most people, including managers, avoid giving candid feedback? It is likely they have learned—from experience that goes all the way back to childhood—that most people react negatively to candid feedback. The recipient may get angry, become defensive, lose motivation, grow less cooperative, or retaliate by saying bad things about the giver. In time, most of us learn to temper our candor, especially when it involves people with whom we expect to have an ongoing relationship. This aversion to candor means that those who want timely, candid feedback usually have to work for it.

What if I Have to Explain Myself?

*"Excuses—don't use them. Your friends don't need
them and your enemies won't believe them."*

—*W. Clement Stone*

At their next lunch Matt told Paula about a few of the challenges
he was facing with one of his projects. They explored strategies
for dealing with the barriers and how to move forward. The discussion inevitably shifted back to the topic of feedback.

"I'm really happy with how the four steps—and priming the
pump—have worked for me," said Matt. "What's most impressive is that Jalee's behavior has improved. By changing how I
receive her feedback, she's actually changed how she gives it,
and all for the better."

"Confucius would be pleased. He was once asked, 'Is it easier
to give criticism or to receive it?' He replied, 'If people knew
how to receive it, it would be easy to give it.' When people feel
stressed about giving someone feedback, the stress reduces their
capacity to think clearly, and they end up doing it poorly. By
using your four-step model you have taken most of the stress out
of the process for Jalee—so she finds it easier to give you helpful
feedback."

"That's good to know, but I'm not sure my model fits all feedback situations."

"Why's that?"

"Well, yesterday, I was in a situation where the four steps didn't
seem appropriate."

"What happened?"

"You know Jim in Accounting? He called and told me I'd gone over budget, which wasn't true. I know I'm not supposed to explain myself, but if I hadn't said something, he would have taken it as an admission of guilt. First, that would have been misleading to him; he would be making decisions based on incorrect data. And second, it could really hurt me if he takes his false information to higher levels."

"What did you say?"

Matt sighed. "I tried to explain the facts, but it didn't do any good."

"Why not?"

"He seemed to block it out. He just kept telling me he had the figures in black and white, and I needed to face reality."

"Okay. Let's look at this from Jim's point of view. When he has to tell someone they've overspent and he's going to shut down their account, what do you think usually happens?"

"There's an argument."

"Right," Paula said. "When ancient armies would go to battle, they didn't take just their weapons—swords and spears—they had defensive tools as well—their shields. When Jim comes in with his numbers, he knows from past experience that he's likely to get into a fight, so his psychological shield is at the ready. When you tell him he's wrong and pull out evidence to prove it, he sees a counterattack. So what does he do with his shield?"

"He raises it."

"Exactly, and suddenly your explanation buys you nothing. The trick isn't just to explain yourself; it's to do it in such a way that you will actually be heard."

"How do I get through his shield, then?"

"You don't. You have to make it safe for him to put his shield down. Which of the steps from your model would help Jim feel respected and safe?"

Matt thought for a moment. "All of the first three steps."

"Right. So did you start by acknowledging the gift?"

"Nope."

"How about opening the gift and digging about to find something of value?"

"You got me there as well. In all honesty, I didn't follow any of the steps. I knew Jim was misinformed, so I assumed that I'd never find any value in his feedback." Matt was silent for a moment, then added, "So you're saying I should follow the first three steps and then when he puts his shield down, I hit him with my sword?" He grinned.

"I know it's tempting," Paula said, smiling back. "Instead, summarize the feedback and ask something like, 'Did I get that right?' If he says no, ask a few more questions to clarify and summarize again. Once he confirms you've understood him completely, then you can offer your side of the story."

"But what if he still refuses to listen?"

"That's unlikely. Most people are reasonably fair-minded. When you make a sincere—and explicit—attempt to understand them, they will almost always listen in return."

"Right. *Almost* always. What if they're not fair-minded?"

"Then you still haven't lost anything because the other person wouldn't have listened to your explanation anyway. In fact, you've actually gained something that could be valuable in the future."

"What's that?" Matt asked.

"Knowledge. By asking questions and listening, you have the clearest understanding of the other person's concerns and their information sources. Now, even if he won't listen to you, at least you have the advantage of being more informed. If the issue then has to be resolved at some higher level, you're better equipped to present your case persuasively.

"Some people find this almost impossible to do. They fear that if they do all the listening, then the other person gets to 'score all the points.' Here's the interesting thing: the harder you try to win an argument, the greater the likelihood you're going to fail—because you'll just end up talking to a shield. Not talking, at least at first, is the single most effective strategy for getting your message across."

"So whether they're fair-minded or not, you think it's to my advantage to go through the first three steps before explaining myself?"

"Definitely," replied Paula. "Also, there's another strategy that is sometimes effective, especially if the situation is emotion-ally charged or you really do believe the other person is being unfair: after going through the first three steps, take a time out by tabling the discussion for a while. Tell the person you value their feedback, you would like to give it more thought, and you'll get back to them. That gives both of you the space to work through your emotions effectively. In that time you can gather data, think about what you've been told and decide—with a cooler head—what the best response might be."

"I can see how doing that could have stopped me from getting defensive. Jim would also have been less likely to get defensive and raise his shield."

"That's exactly what your first three steps are designed to do. Then, after a day or two, or whenever you've managed to work through your emotions and feel ready to talk, you can go back. Restart the conversation by thanking the other person for their feedback and summarizing the previous discussion.

"If you use this strategy, however, I do have one word of caution: don't defer the conversation to avoid dealing with a tough issue."

"Agreed," Matt said. "But what if it's an urgent issue that really needs to be dealt with immediately?"

"In that case, you may have to explain yourself in that same conversation. But only do so after you're sure you understand the other person and they confirm you understand—in other words, after Step 3. But whenever you have the luxury of time and can wait before responding, do it later. It's a lot more effective."

"I'll try it with Jim. At this point I have nothing to lose."

"What will you say?"

"I'll start with an apology for getting defensive," Matt said. "That should help him lower his shield right away. Next, I'll tell him I've spent a lot of time trying to get things clear in my own mind since our last conversation, and I'll ask him if he'd mind helping me."

"And then?"

"Then I'll get back to Step 3: summarize my understanding of his concerns and ask if I've got it right. Once he agrees that I've understood him, he'll probably be more willing to listen to me."

"That sounds good. Actually, based on what you've said, I'm wondering if my earlier statement about not explaining yourself is complete. After Step 2, perhaps it should say, 'Don't explain yourself—at least, not until Step 3, after you understand the feedback and the other person feels understood.'"

Paula pulled out her copy of Matt's model and penned the changes to Steps 2 and 3.

Four Steps to Receiving the Gift of Feedback

   1. Acknowledge the Gift.

   2. Open the Gift.

>   Do NOT explain yourself—**at least not until Step 3, after you understand the feedback and the other person feels understood.**

   3. Confirm the Nature and Value of the Gift.

>   Put into words what you understand the gift to be **and ask if you understood it correctly**.

   4. Use the Gift.

Matt studied his model.

"You know," he said, "it just dawned on me how important that first step really is, especially the part about assuming you're going to find something of value. If you think there's a bomb in the package, you'll never open it and you'll never find the gift. If I had assumed that Jim was trying to be helpful with his feedback, I may have learned more from it."

"Exactly. That's why we need to give the benefit of the doubt to those who offer us feedback. It's like forgiveness. When one person forgives another, it's usually the person doing the forgiving who stands to gain the most. When you assume the feedback giver truly wants to be helpful, that assumption benefits you more than it benefits them."

"I feel like I'm about ready to talk to Jim again. Thanks for your help. I'll let you know how it goes."

Paula smiled. "I look forward to hearing about it."

When Matt returned to his office, he pulled out his journal and updated the four-step process with the changes he and Paula had discussed. Afterward, he added three more principles:

> **If you want to be heard, make it safe for the other person to lower their shield. Stop talking and start listening.**

> **Take a time out if you need to think through what you've been told or need time to get your defensiveness under control.**

> **When you assume the feedback giver wants to give you something of value, that assumption is more for your benefit than it is for theirs.**

The next morning, after thinking more deeply about how to approach the situation, Matt dropped by Jim's office. Jim didn't appear very happy to see him.

"Jim," said Matt, "I want to apologize for how I reacted yesterday. I'm sorry I got defensive. You were only doing your job."

Jim didn't respond, so Matt continued. "I'd really like to understand this, so it doesn't happen again. If now's a good time, could you walk me through your numbers again and clarify the next steps we need to take?"

Jim still looked a little wary, but a hint of cautious optimism crept into his voice. "Now's as good a time as any," he said. "Here's the issue…"

Matt followed the steps very carefully. He had even scripted in advance some of the things he wanted to say and the questions he planned to ask. While Jim responded to Matt's questions, Matt made sure to ask himself:

> Where's the gift?
>
> What can I learn from this?
>
> What did I do or say that may have created this misperception?
>
> What can I do to ensure this doesn't happen again?

As Matt listened, it gradually occurred to him that Jim might be missing two critical reports he had written.

"Do you have my reports of June 15 and July 1?" asked Matt.

Jim quickly checked his file. "No," he replied.

Matt was tempted to criticize Jim for not getting all the facts before jumping to a conclusion, but he knew that would simply prompt Jim to raise his shield.

"Jim," Matt said, "I'm sorry. It seems that I failed to get you all the reports you needed. I think they may explain the discrepancy."

Matt retrieved the reports and they reviewed them together. In a matter of minutes they had resolved the issue and cleared up the misunderstanding. Matt gained an important insight from the conversation. After returning to his office, he added it to his list:

When you are convinced the other person has a misperception of you or your performance, the gift lies in discovering—and admitting—your role in creating that misperception.

The Price of Defensiveness

"I once had a salesperson who was an expert at dealing with customer objections. He got sales, and hence rewards, when he did a good job of 'overcoming objections.' Unfortunately, I couldn't get through to him because he treated all feedback as objections to be overcome, and he did it very well. In the end I got tired of not making progress with him—so I let him go."

—A Targeted Learning Client

Criticism is not an invitation to defend one's ideas or actions. It's an invitation to understand things more deeply, to see potential flaws that one cannot see without the corrective lens of feedback.

John Templeton observed, "Only through humility can you achieve great understanding." People who lack humility want to be right. As with this salesperson, they view concerns, suggestions and criticism as objections to be overcome. People with big egos may win arguments, but they lose customers and potential allies.

You Think You're Better Than Us

"I'm by nature very introverted, which has created some difficulties for me in my career. The most serious problem surfaced a year or so after I was promoted to management. As with many managers, I was promoted not because of my superior interpersonal or leadership skills, but because I had the best technical skills.

"After becoming a manager, I continued to do what I did best, which was to solve technical problems. And I avoided things that made me feel uncomfortable, which included interacting with people on an informal and personal basis. One day I received feedback from some direct reports. They essentially said, 'You're unapproachable and elitist. You think you're better than us.'

"I couldn't believe it. I thought they must be describing someone else. If anything, I've often felt inferior to others, particularly those who seemed so comfortable in social settings. Instead of seeing my behavior for what it was—evidence of my shy and introverted nature—they interpreted it as evidence that I thought I was better than them. Because the feedback was based on misperceptions, I thought it wasn't valid and was therefore inclined to dismiss it. But eventually I came to see that although their view of me was based on a misperception, it was that view that was undermining our relationship and their willingness to give me their best efforts. The gift to me was discovering that people didn't react to me based on who I was—shy and introverted—but based on their perception of who I was—aloof and elitist.

"I have often heard the phrase, 'Perception is reality,' but not until this happened did I understand what that really meant. Their perceptions of me were creating the reality of an ineffective team. If I wanted a different reality, one that involved an effective and collaborative team, I would have to change those perceptions. That would require me to get out of my comfort zone, spend more time interacting with team members, and sometimes talking about personal interests. I will never be a charismatic leader, but because of that feedback I'm a much more effective manager."

—A participant in Targeted Learning's "Seeking and Receiving Feedback" Workshop

What we can learn from this case is that subjective perceptions, even when they're inaccurate, are more powerful in shaping behavior than so-called objective facts. In order to save his career, this leader had to discard the erroneous notion that "facts trump perceptions."

As Paula said, "If you're diligent, smart and honest, your career is more likely to be derailed by inaccurate perceptions than by accurate ones."

A Few Years Later

"Successful people are those who can lay a firm foundation with the bricks that others throw at them."

– David Brinkley

Paula ended up taking a promotion elsewhere in the company. Matt quickly distinguished himself as one of the organization's rising stars. In time, he was asked to be a mentor.

One morning when Matt arrived at work, Beth, his new mentee, was already standing outside his office. "Hey, I could use your help," she said. "My supervisor, Kathy, hardly gives me any feedback. Then when she does, it's a huge dump session and often it's so late there's nothing I can do about it. At this point I don't know if I can trust her to tell me anything useful."

"Well, let's draw it out," Matt said, taking a sheet of scratch paper from his desk. "First tell me about some of your experiences with Kathy's feedback and how you responded to it." While Beth explained, Matt's pen ran rampant across the paper. Beth noticed and her voice trailed off. "Don't worry," he said. "I'm just summarizing what you're telling me so we can look at it from every possible angle. Keep going; it'll help me capture things more accurately."

Throughout Beth's account Matt asked questions to uncover additional detail. When he felt he understood the situation, he finished his notes and pushed them toward Beth. "Take a look at this. Does it accurately capture what's happening?"

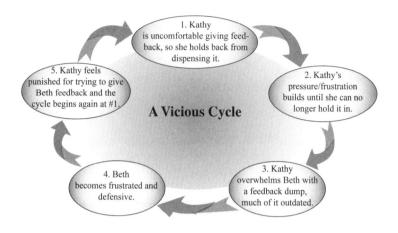

Beth studied the paper and sighed. "You've captured it."

"Who's feeding this cycle?" Matt asked.

"Both of us," Beth admitted.

"Now that you've seen the cycle and you know what's happening, who's in the best position to break it?"

"I don't like where this is going." Beth frowned, then continued, "I suppose I'm in the best position, because I recognize what's happening. Still, she's the boss, so she has more power to change it than I do."

"It's true that she has more formal power. So how has waiting for her to use that power more productively been working for you?"

Beth nodded in resignation. "I get your point. I need to make the first move."

"How do you plan to do it?"

"There's got to be some way to convince her that I *want* her feedback and that she doesn't have to bottle it up. But to do that I need to get over my own knee-jerk defensiveness. In all honesty, my reactions are usually triggered by the fact that she's giving me feedback too late to be of any use. Since I can't change the past, I feel like I have to defend it."

"That's a great insight. So what will you do to help Kathy get into the habit of giving more regular and timely feedback?"

"I could go to her and ask for feedback rather than waiting for her to come to me. And I should probably listen to her feedback without getting defensive, regardless of what she says."

"I think that'll work," Matt replied. He gave Beth a few thoughts about asking for specific feedback, as well as priming the pump if necessary.

"Sometimes when you ask for feedback, you get more than you bargained for," said Matt. "So whatever you do, don't take offense. People who take offense come across as insecure or as having a chip on their shoulder. You know what my dad used to say about people who have chips on their shoulders? 'A chip on the shoulder is a sure sign of wood higher up.'"

Beth smiled, "I hope you haven't seen any chips on my shoulders."

"None at all," laughed Matt. "Be sure to let me know how your conversation goes with Kathy."

Matt returned to his desk and considered the discussion with Beth. One of the nice things about being a mentor, he thought, is that you often learn as much from your mentee as they do from you.

Matt opened his journal and reviewed his list of principles for receiving feedback. He reflected on his experiences and saw how a few small changes had lead to great gains.

Having re-familiarized himself with his notes about receiving feedback, Matt summarized his ideas in a single thought:

> *The value of feedback depends less on the ability of others to give it well than it does on our ability to receive it well.*

The Crumbling Cookie

Wally Amos, founder of the Famous Amos Cookie Company, opened his first cookie store in Los Angeles, California, in 1975. In the first year he sold $300,000 worth of cookies. In the second year, sales exceeded $1,000,000. By 1982 his annual sales reached $12 million with his cookies available in 20,000 locations, including supermarkets. This rampant growth came crashing down in the mid 80s and Wally Amos lost his company. Later he identified the cause of his corporate misfortunes.

"I thought I knew more than anyone else...I wasn't listening to other people. Teamwork—that is the greatest lesson I learned from losing Famous Amos... It's not about me, Wally Amos. It's about respecting the rest of my team members...giving them access to make suggestions."

Feedback has many synonyms, including suggestion, input, advice, criticism, condemnation and even insult. Whatever you choose to call it, feedback is essential to learning faster and avoiding disaster.

Leo Buscaglia observed, "The worst sin in the world is going to bed at night as stupid as you were in the morning." Seeking and being open to feedback allows you to efficiently gather the teachings of each day as it goes by, so you will always go to bed a little wiser than you were the day before.

The Battle of Isandlwana

On January 22, 1879, the British army suffered its greatest defeat ever at the hands of an army equipped with primitive weapons. A British battalion, equipped with artillery and modern Martini-Henry rifles, was effectively wiped out by a Zulu force armed with short stabbing spears, clubs and cowhide shields. The engagement came to be known as the Battle of Isandlwana.

As the sun set that day, approximately 3,000 warriors and soldiers lay slain on the field of battle. What stunned the British was that 1,329 of the dead were their own. Only fifty British enlisted men and five of their officers escaped.

How did an army equipped with artillery and rifles capable of firing ten rounds a minute lose almost as many men as an army equipped with clubs and stabbing spears? Even if the British were appalling marksmen—which they were not—and their bullets found their targets only one time in ten, they had the firepower necessary to inflict over 1,000 casualties a minute.

On the morning of the 20th, two days before that fateful battle, the British arrived at Isandlwana and set up a forward camp. The British commander, Lord Chelmsford, decided that there was no need to entrench his forces or even take the rudimentary defensive step of circling the wagons.

Early on the 22nd the British dispatched a scouting party who soon stumbled on a small group of Zulu warriors. The scouts chased this group into a dry river course, only to discover the main Zulu force of about 20,000 sitting in total silence. The Zulus had planned to launch their attack on the 23rd, but upon being discovered they went immediately on the offensive.

An officer arriving from another battalion gave the following account of the last stage of the battle from his safe vantage point atop a nearby hill:

> "In a few seconds we distinctly saw the guns [artillery pieces] fired again, one after the other, sharp. This was done several times—a pause, and then a flash-flash! The sun was shining on the camp at the time, and then the camp looked dark, just as if a shadow was passing over it. The guns did not fire after that, and in a few minutes all the [British] tents had disappeared."[1]

Tactical surprise and numerical superiority do not adequately explain how the Zulu army totally overwhelmed the British. Equipped with superior weaponry, the British battalion had the capacity to easily defeat a Zulu army of 40,000, let alone 20,000. Furthermore, the initial distance between the main Zulu force and the British granted the latter enough time to move into an effective battle formation. As was typical for the British at the time, they chose to fight in a linear formation—a disastrous decision which made it easier for the Zulu warriors to utilize their speed and numerical superiority to outflank and overwhelm the British.[2]

On the surface, this British disaster was the result of two poor decisions: the failure to establish an adequate initial defense, and the subsequent choice of a linear battle formation upon engagement. The more fundamental reason, however, was the failure of the British officers to seek and heed the input of their local scouts.

The scouts, British subjects of European descent, had lived on the South African frontier for most—or all—of their lives. They understood the Zulu military strategies and their strengths. They were familiar with the battle tactics that earlier

Dutch settlers had used to defeat Zulu armies that sometimes outnumbered them more than twenty to one. The scouts also respected the fighting capabilities of the Zulus. The British officers, on the other hand, grossly underestimated the discipline, motivation, speed, stealth and superb leadership of the Zulu army.

The critical question is, why did the British officers choose not to seek or listen to the expert advice of the colonial scouts? In a word: arrogance.

The British saw the colonial scouts as ill-mannered, poorly-educated drunks. A sense of superiority rendered the British officers incapable of accepting feedback from these less refined, less educated subordinates.

What the officers failed to understand was that the colonial scouts were in fact very well educated—not in the classrooms of elite British schools or military academies, but in the grass-lands and bush of Africa.

How often, in organizations across the globe, do individuals and groups make disastrous mistakes because their egos prevent them from accepting feedback from those who are different from them, or from those who occupy positions of lower status or power? How often do insecure leaders view criticism as a threat to their authority rather than as a surer, shorter path to success?

It's unlikely that you will ever have to risk your life in war. Nevertheless, the lessons of Isandlwana remain indispensable to your career and your business. To avoid making poor decisions—decisions that could undermine your career or the well-being of your company—you need to be open to feedback from those around you, regardless of their education, background, experience level or culture. It is easy to learn from the criticism of people we hold in high esteem and from those who are skilled communicators. What takes real skill and wisdom is to profit from the counsel of those we don't admire, and from the rough and tumble "scouts" in our own lives. As noted by Publilius Syrus, "Many receive advice, only the wise profit from it."

[1] F.E. Colenso, *History of the Zulu War and its Origin*, London, 1880.
[2] Ian Knight, *Isandlwana 1879: The Great Zulu Victory*, Osprey, 2002.

Feedback and You

"Look upon the man who tells thee thy faults as if he told thee of a hidden treasure."

—*The Dhammapada*

The higher you ascend in your professional life—in terms of performance, title, status, rank or reputation—the less likely you are to receive direct, unfiltered feedback.[1] Most people find it difficult to speak truth to power or to those who are recognized experts. So remember, the more your performance (or that of your company) resembles world-class performance, the more diligent you need to be in seeking and receiving the gift of feedback.

If you are a leader, you have a responsibility to inoculate yourself and those around you against the fear of criticism. This is crucial because competitive advantage comes from new ideas, and those new ideas come from people. But the fear of criticism smothers promising new ideas in the cradle. It drives people to say nothing original and persuades them to do nothing bold.

One of our favorite quotes comes from Abraham Maslow, the famous psychological theorist. He said, "It's a great sign of respect to me if someone feels I'm strong enough and capable enough and objective enough to tell me when I've done or said something stupid. It's only those who regard me as delicate, sensitive, weak or fragile who will not dare to disagree with me."

In essence, honest criticism is the highest form of praise. It says that you're an adult; you can handle the truth and you have the capacity to grow.

Henry David Thoreau observed, "People don't give you their most effective criticism until you provoke them. Severe truth is expressed with some bitterness." Because most people avoid conflict and want to be liked, they tend to tell you the unvarnished truth only when they are frustrated or downright angry. As a consequence, the truth will not always come across tactfully. Remember, the next time you get candid feedback from someone who appears angry or frustrated, be grateful for those emotions. Without them, the giver may never have found the courage to level with you.

We recently conducted a significant study in which we correlated people's pay with their attitudes toward feedback. We found that those who were open to criticism in any form—who didn't put preconditions on it, who didn't say people had to be constructive or polite—earned significantly more money than those who said they were open to criticism as long as it was "constructive."

One reason for this correlation is that people who are open to the gift of criticism, no matter how it's wrapped, get more unfiltered information. With better information, they make better decisions. Better decisions lead to better work results and more satisfied customers. And in organizations that pay for performance, having more satisfied customers leads to higher pay.

The problem with making openness to criticism conditional upon it being "constructive" is that only the receiver gets to define what "constructive" means. Despite the best of intentions, tact and skill on the part of the feedback giver, if the receiver doesn't like what they hear, they simply label the feedback "unconstructive." The recipient then claims to have a legitimate reason to dismiss it.

What a weak excuse. In our experience, the person who says he is open to criticism as long as it's constructive really doesn't want any criticism at all.

In our story, Matt came to the conclusion that the value of feedback depends less on the ability of others to give it well than it does on our ability to receive it well. This requires a major paradigm shift for modern organizations. The prevailing attitude assumes that the value of feedback depends on how well the giver frames and delivers it, so organizations continue to invest heavily in teaching managers how to initiate and handle difficult conversations. These conversations, however, continue to go poorly because most people don't know how to receive feedback as a gift.

There is another reason the prevailing paradigm is counter-productive. When one person gives another feedback, the receiver stands to gain the most; they benefit from additional information and have the opportunity to improve themselves. The giver, on the other hand, is the one taking the greatest risk; it could blow up in their face and permanently damage a valued relationship. If the receiver has the most to gain and the giver the most to lose, why should the bulk of the burden to "do it right" fall on the giver? Although we believe that responsibility for the effectiveness of feedback is shared, the duty falls primarily on the receiver.

Let's restate the new paradigm one more time:

> **The value of feedback depends less on the ability of others to give it well than it does on our ability to receive it well.**

Think of it this way: if the value of the feedback we receive depends on the ability of others to give it well, then our growth and success is in their hands. When we accept that the value of the feedback depends on how we receive it, our growth and success is in our own hands.

Now that's a liberating concept.

The principles and techniques in this book were presented in the context of using feedback to make smarter business decisions, avoid costly mistakes, and to learn more and faster from your work experience. Although the focus was on becoming more successful in the workplace, the concepts apply to every aspect of life. Some of the most gratifying feedback we have ever received has been from people who told us how these principles helped them in their personal and family lives.

We wish you the best in applying the lessons from this book. May you find the gift in all feedback and experience the joy of going to bed each night a little wiser than you were the day before.

[1] J.R. Kofodimos, R.E. Kaplan, and W.H. Drath, *"Beyond Ambition,"* Jossey Bass, 1991.

Additional Resources

Summary of Feedback Principles

Realities about Feedback
You can't solve problems you don't see. Feedback gives you additional pairs of eyes. It's a really bad sign if you make a mistake and no one criticizes you. The most unhelpful feedback is no feedback at all. Feedback is a gift—even when it's inaccurate. You don't have to agree with feedback to benefit from it. You only have to understand it.

Principles for Seeking Feedback
When asking for feedback, be specific about what you want and why you want it. Be ready to prime the pump with a self-critique.

Principles for Receiving Feedback

Feedback is a gift, so treat it as such.

Don't discard the gift because you don't like the wrapping.

Don't reject the gift simply because you don't like or respect the giver—or because you suspect their motives.

It may be more comfortable working with diplomats, but you learn a lot more from straight talkers.

Take a time out if you need to think through what you've been told or if you need time to get your defensiveness under control.

If you want to be heard, make it safe for the other person to lower their shield. Stop talking and start listening.

To find the gift, ask yourself questions such as:

Where's the gift?

What can I learn from this?

What did I do or say that may have created this misperception?

What can I do to ensure this doesn't happen again?

Continue asking these questions until you find the gift.

When you encounter inaccurate information, unfair conclusions, etc., examine it carefully, set it aside—along with your own prejudices—and keep digging.

When you are convinced the other person has a misperception of you or your performance, the gift lies in discovering—and admitting—your role in creating that misperception.

When you assume the feedback giver wants to give you something of value, that assumption is more for your benefit than it is for theirs.

You can set feedback aside, but only after giving it due diligence.

If feedback comes with the expectation that you will take action, you do have the right to set it aside, but you still need to let the person know your decision—and how you arrived at it.

Four Steps to Receiving the Gift of Feedback

1. **Acknowledge the Gift.**

   Say thank you; give the giver the benefit of the doubt.

   Assume there is something of value.

2. **Open the Gift.**

   Sometimes the gift is hard to find; it takes digging.

   To find it, ask lots of questions and listen with an open mind.

   Do NOT explain yourself—at least not until Step 3, after you understand the feedback and the other person feels understood.

3. **Confirm the Nature and Value of the Gift.**

   Put into words what you understand the gift to be and ask if you understood it correctly.

   If you can, mention how you plan to use it.

   Thank the person again and ask, "Is there anything else I could do to be more effective in the future?"

4. **Use the Gift.**

   After using it—and experiencing its benefits—let the giver know how it helped you.

   If you can't use the gift right now, say "thank you" and set it aside; you might find a use for it later.

   Before setting feedback aside, check in with someone you trust who will be honest with you.

Getting Connected

Visit Our Website

To learn more about how Targeted Learning and the authors can help you or your company achieve world-class performance, go to: www.targetedlearning.com

Subscribe to Our Free E-Newsletter

Be the first to hear about the latest research, fresh insights and practical tools for expanding your impact at work. Get on the list for our free e-newsletter by going to: www.targetedlearning.com/nl

Get Quality Discounts

To order more copies of "Where's the Gift?" or any of our other titles, please call us at 801-235-9414 or go to www.targetedlearning.com/books. Volume discounts are available for orders of 10 or more books.

Other titles available from Targeted Learning:

The Beyond Job Satisfaction Fieldbook: Tools and Templates for Maximizing Your Engagement and Vitality at Work
Building Communities of Learning: How to Harness the Collective Genius of the People in Your Organization

To contact Targeted Learning: **Call us at 801-235-9414 or email:**
                                     info@targetedlearning.com

To contact the authors: **nigel@targetedlearning.com**
                                     mj@targetedlearning.com

Learning More

Our Goals at Targeted Learning are:

1. To help organizations achieve world-class performance by fully engaging the talents and energies of their people, and,
2. To help individuals learn faster, work smarter and achieve more.

Workshops

- The Feedback Formula
- The 7 Conversations for Exceptional Leaders
- The 7 Conversations for High-Impact Individuals
- How to Influence Others When You Are Not In Charge
- Leadership Skills for Technical Professionals
- Mentoring Skills
- Coaching for Superior Performance
- Mastering My Career (classroom or online versions available)
- Career Leadership Skills
- Powerful Presentations

Consulting and Speaking Engagements

The authors, as well as other Targeted Learning speakers and consultants, are available to speak and consult in the areas of:

- Leadership
- Talent Development and Retention
- Career Management
- Total Employee Engagement
- Receiving and Giving Feedback
- Coaching Skills
- Performance Management
- Influence without Authority
- Mentoring Skills

Dealing with Psychological Bullies

> *"When angry, count to ten before you speak; if very angry, 100."*
> —*Thomas Jefferson*

Our advice to treat all feedback as a gift should not be misconstrued to suggest that:

1.   You need to put up with abuse from psychological bullies, or,

2.   We are giving license to people to give feedback any way they please.

A few people we've met in our workshops on seeking and receiving feedback have asked, "What do you do if there is someone around you who is constantly giving feedback in a way that is clearly designed to hurt, not help?" Name calling, shouting and threats—explicit or implied—all fall into the category of abusive feedback.

We know from our research that honest feedback will often hurt, no matter the intent or how carefully it is delivered. We also know that psychological bullies exist. To submit to abuse is to invite more. By treating abusive feedback as a gift one could unwittingly "feed the monster," which only makes matters worse.

Some psychological bullies are emotional sadists. They take pleasure in causing emotional pain. When you respond to their feedback without flinching—when you refuse to be intimidated—you deprive them of their satisfaction. At this point, they will often take their bullying elsewhere.

On the other hand, some psychological bullies have a pathological need to control or dominate others. These bullies will see your composure as a challenge to their dominance and they may increase the pressure before eventually backing off.

Finally, some people who appear to be psychological bullies are simply insecure individuals who lack sophisticated social skills. They mistakenly believe that the only way they can get others to cooperate is to threaten or intimidate them. These people need to be taught that respect and tact are more likely to foster cooperation than verbal assaults are.

Psychological bullies will often justify their behavior by presenting themselves as paragons of openness and honesty. The truth is, there is no real difference between them and the common schoolyard bully. They use words rather than fists to dominate or inflict pain, but their intent remains the same.

There are three options for dealing with the psychological bully:

1. Receive the feedback using the four-step process we recommend. This approach shows that you can't be intimidated and honors the principle to "assume their motive is to be helpful." Treating their feedback as a gift may be enough to bring about the change, especially if they are socially inept rather than true psychological bullies. (Their intent all along may have been to be genuinely helpful. It is possible they simply lacked the necessary interpersonal skills, or they didn't comprehend the negative impact of their delivery style.) If this approach doesn't work, move to options 2 or 3.

2. Coach them on how they can increase their influence by giving more effective feedback:

- Begin a conversation with the offending party by explaining that you want to have a good working relationship with them and that you want to learn from their feedback.

- Acknowledge that you believe their intent in giving you feedback is to help you be more successful, which is why you're having this conversation.

- Explain that you sometimes find it difficult to be responsive to their feedback because of how it's delivered. Be specific about the aspects of the delivery that get in the way of you learning from their feedback.

- Follow with suggestions on how they can make it easier for you to learn from and respond positively to their feedback.

- End by asking them if they would be willing in the future to give you feedback in the way you described. If they say "yes," thank them, and be sure to acknowledge their first efforts to be more helpful—even if they don't pull it off perfectly. If, however, it becomes clear that they refuse to honor your request, you may need to move to option 3.

These first two options build on a principle expressed by Napoleon Bonaparte: "Never ascribe to malice, that which can be explained by incompetence."

3. The failure of the first two approaches may confirm that the person truly is a psychological bully. If that is the case, get out of the abusive relationship as soon as you can. This might include a multitude of different actions, including getting a transfer, quitting your job, seeking help (e.g., from

a manager or HR professional), or simply avoiding contact with the bully. Most companies today realize how toxic a hostile work environment is to employee morale and retention, and will not treat bullying lightly. If options 1 and 2 don't work with a manager or co-worker, consider going to HR or up the chain of command with your concerns. If the person is a psychological bully, then there will be others in the organization who are experiencing the same things you are, and you will have done the entire organization a big favor by exposing the bully and the hostile work environment they are creating.

Notwithstanding the above recommendation, we recognize that within a few shortsighted organizations, bullies are tolerated if they achieve significant short-term results. These bullies pump up short-term profits by liquidating the human assets of the organization at a fraction of its true value. If senior leaders cannot or will not see this behavior for what it really is, or if they exhibit it themselves, update your resume and start looking for a new job.

Finally, if you are in a personal relationship with someone who is psychologically or physically abusive, seek professional counseling and help.

You Don't Have to Take It

"At a previous company I had a manager who often shouted at employees, but for some reason I escaped his wrath for a long time. Then one day he started yelling at me. I was caught off guard and had no idea how to respond. Finally I stood, said, 'I can't take this,' and walked out of his office. The next day he came to me and apologized. He never shouted at me again, although he continued to shout at everyone else."

—Boeing participant in Targeted
Learning's Influence Skills Workshop

It is important to note that this manager continued to bully others in the office, but not the woman who refused to submit to his abuse. As William Hazlitt observed, "The way to procure insults is to submit to them."

Taking Action

Our goal in writing this book was not to simply entertain or educate, but to inspire action. Now that you know how to receive all feedback as a gift, it's time to act.

> *"I have been impressed with the urgency of doing. Knowing is not enough; we must apply. Being willing is not enough; we must do."*
>
> —*Leonardo da Vinci*

Part A: Selecting Those You Should Ask

Seek feedback from anyone who has first-hand insights about you or your work. In doing so, remember this observation by Confucius: "He cannot help me. He agrees with everything I say." Select people who are likely to be candid and whose perspectives will help you learn about yourself and your growth opportunities:

___ manager/supervisor	___ spouse
___ customers	___ children
___ business partners	___ parents
___ manager's manager	___ friends
___ direct reports	___ teachers
___ peers or colleagues	___ coaches
___ team members	___ mentors
___ family	___ other(s)

List the names of at least five potential feedback givers:

_____
_____
_____

Part B: Deciding When to Ask

Effective feedback is ongoing. It should become a part of your continuous improvement program. Below are some occasions when you may wish to seek feedback:

- When you need a sounding board for your ideas or proposals.

- At key milestones and the completion of projects.

- When the body language or comments of others suggest they have concerns.

- When you have concerns or are uncertain about your impact on others.

- Prior to, during, and after team meetings, presentations, etc.

- When there is a change in job expectations or customer commitments.

- When you are looking for new growth opportunities.

Identify at least two people who could give you helpful feedback *within the next week.*

_____

_____

Seek Feedback Sooner as Well as Later

Seeking feedback on a speech after you've delivered it, or on a report post-submission, will enable you to avoid repeating your mistakes.

Far more useful, however, is seeking feedback on your report or speech before you deliver it. We call this "feedforward." Feedforward is defined in the New Oxford American Dictionary as "the modification or control of a process using its anticipated results and effects." In other words, feedforward is information that helps you make improvements to something before it really matters or can hurt you. Feedback can prevent you from repeating mistakes. Feed*forward* helps you avoid making those mistakes in the first place.

What are some opportunities for you to get feedforward?
(e.g., on future presentations, reports, proposals,
new ideas, etc.) _____

_____

_____

Part C: Preparing to Receive Feedback

This exercise will help you prepare to receive feedback.

Who—Identify one person from whom you'd like to receive feedback as soon as possible. _____

When—When will you ask for this feedback? (Identify a specific time or situation in which you will ask.)_____

_____

How—How will you ask for the feedback? (Be specific and be prepared to prime the pump.)

1. What do you want feedback about? (Be specific.)_____

_____
_____

2. Why do you need this feedback? How will it help you, the company, the team or the customer?_____

_____
_____

3. How will you state your request? (Be specific.)_____

_____
_____

4. Is this person likely to resist giving you frank feedback? If so, how might you overcome this resistance? (For example, what specific self-critique could you use to prime the pump?)_____

_____
_____

Part D: Asking For Feedback

1. Ask people who:
    a. are appropriately informed, and
    b. will be candid with you.

2. Be specific about both (a) what you need help with and (b) why it is important to you.

3. Make it worthwhile by explaining the business need or the "WIIFT." (What's in it for them?)

4. Make it safe for the giver to be candid by:
    a. Asking for help, advice or suggestions rather than feedback.
    b. Priming the pump with a self-critique.
    c. Stressing your commitment to being open.
    d. Asking for "feedforward" rather than "feedback." (See the definition on p. 86 of "feedforward.")

Remember: No matter how people respond to your requests, always treat their feedback as a gift. As Edmund Burke said, "He that wrestles with us strengthens our nerves and sharpens our skill. Our antagonist is our helper."

Part E: Using the Gift

Peter Drucker counseled, "Follow effective action with quiet reflection. From the quiet reflection will come more effective action." After you have taken action to get feedback, complete this exercise.

1. Did you find a gift? Yes _____ No _____

2a. If yes, what did you do that helped you find the gift?
    _____

2b. If not, what could you have done differently to find the gift? _____

3. What did you learn about the process of receiving feedback? _____
    _____

4. What did you learn from the content of the feedback itself?
    _____

5. What should you do based on the feedback you received?
    _____

6. Who can help you clarify the feedback, or find the gift in the feedback if you haven't found it? How can they help?
    _____

7. Who can support you in your effort to grow/change based on the feedback? How can they help? _____

Giving Feedback

*"The truth you speak doth lack some gentleness. You rub
the sore when you should bring the plaster."*

—*William Shakespeare*

Under no circumstances do we want our message, "Treat all
feedback as a gift," to be interpreted as absolving the feedback
giver of responsibility to deliver it with consideration and respect
for the recipient. The act of giving feedback carries an obligation
to serve the recipient's interests, not the giver's. Feedback should
never be motivated by a desire to vent, shame or punish; the only
justification for giving feedback is to provide information that
helps people align their actions with their goals.

Giving effective feedback requires one to appropriately balance
tact and candor. The harder the truth to be delivered, the greater
the need to measure one's words and moderate one's tone.

William Penn said it best: "They have the right to censure who
have the heart to help. Those who correct out of anger foster
revenge rather than repentance."

**To access free tips and tools for giving more effective feed-
back, go to www.targetedlearning.com/resources**

Acknowledgements

First and foremost, we'd like to thank our respective spouses, Beverley and Susan. They were energetic editors through countless drafts, and provided steady love and encouragement over the long months of writing and rewriting.

Special thanks also to: Brent Barclay, Conor Patrick, Davilyn Ferrin, Shayne Clarke, Beth Wilkins, Debi Buckner and Shelley Ouderkirk for their priceless feedback; to Sandy DuToit and Heidi Lawson for preparing the book for publication; to Candice and Samantha of BristowJones Marketing for their work on the cover and for taking our feedback so well.

Finally, our gratitude goes out to our client organizations and the thousands of participants who over the years have allowed us to gather valuable data, helped us refine our strategies and principles, and shared their success stories.